A Colouring
Book of
Carnival Costumes

Dandi Palmer

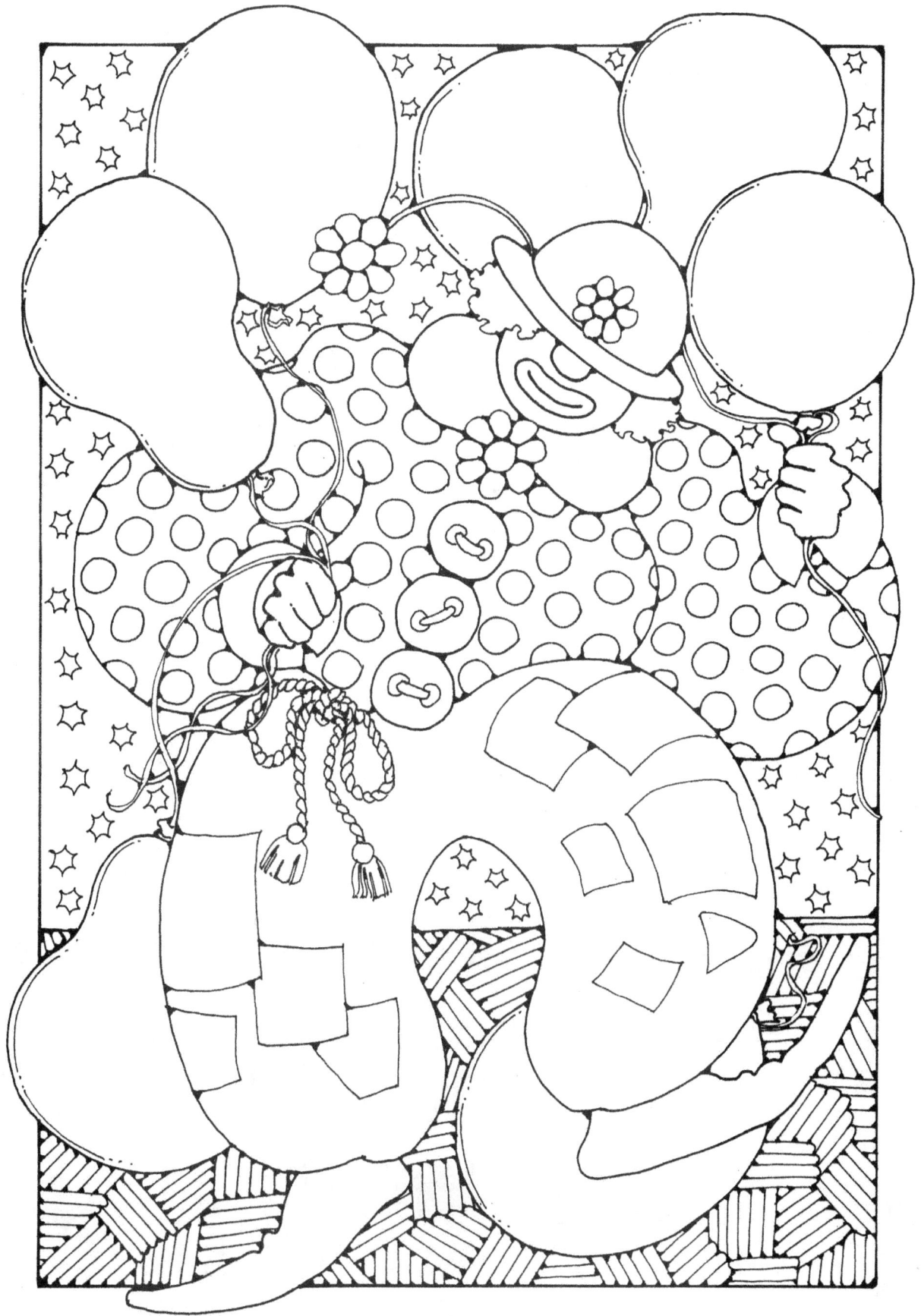

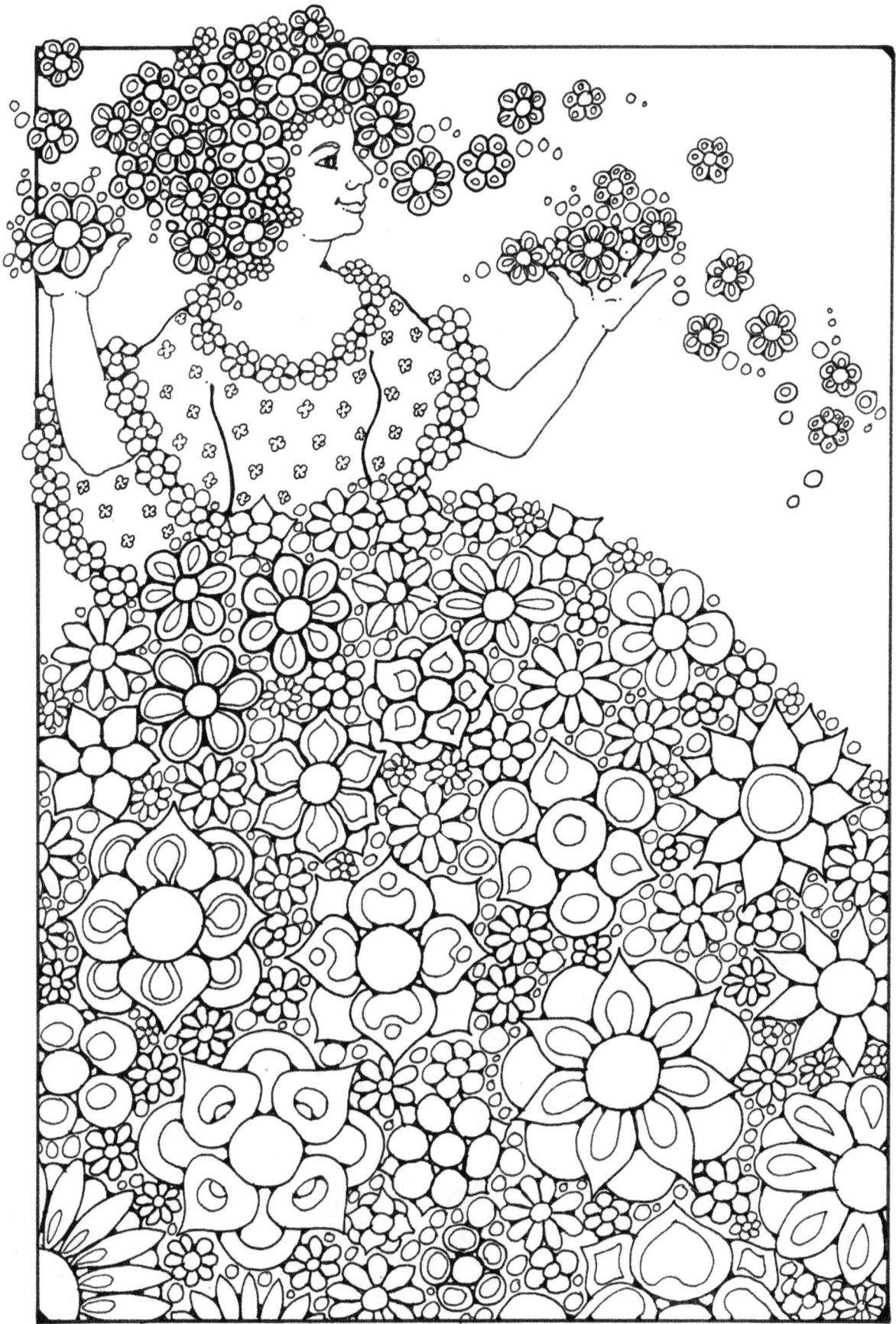

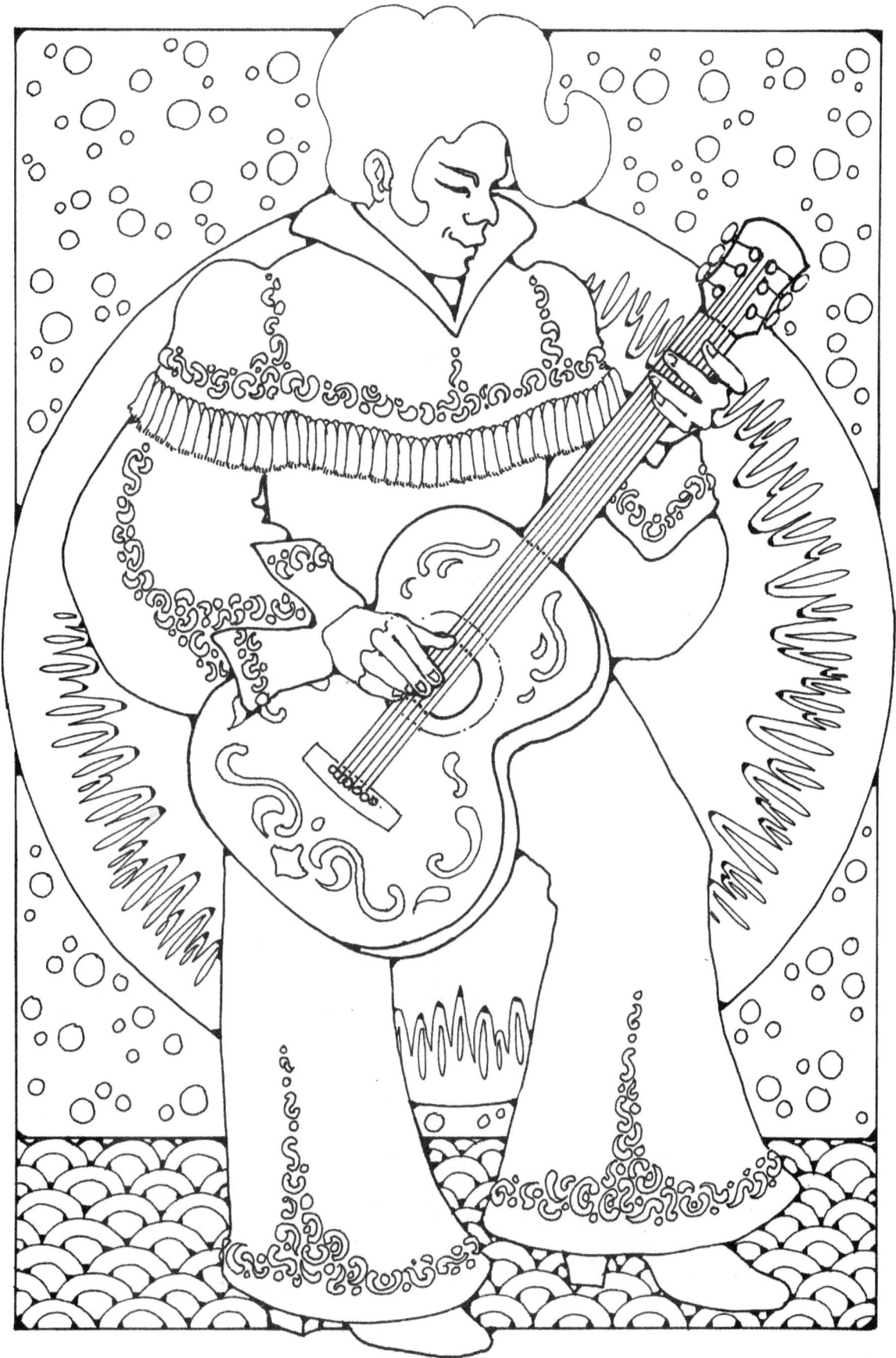

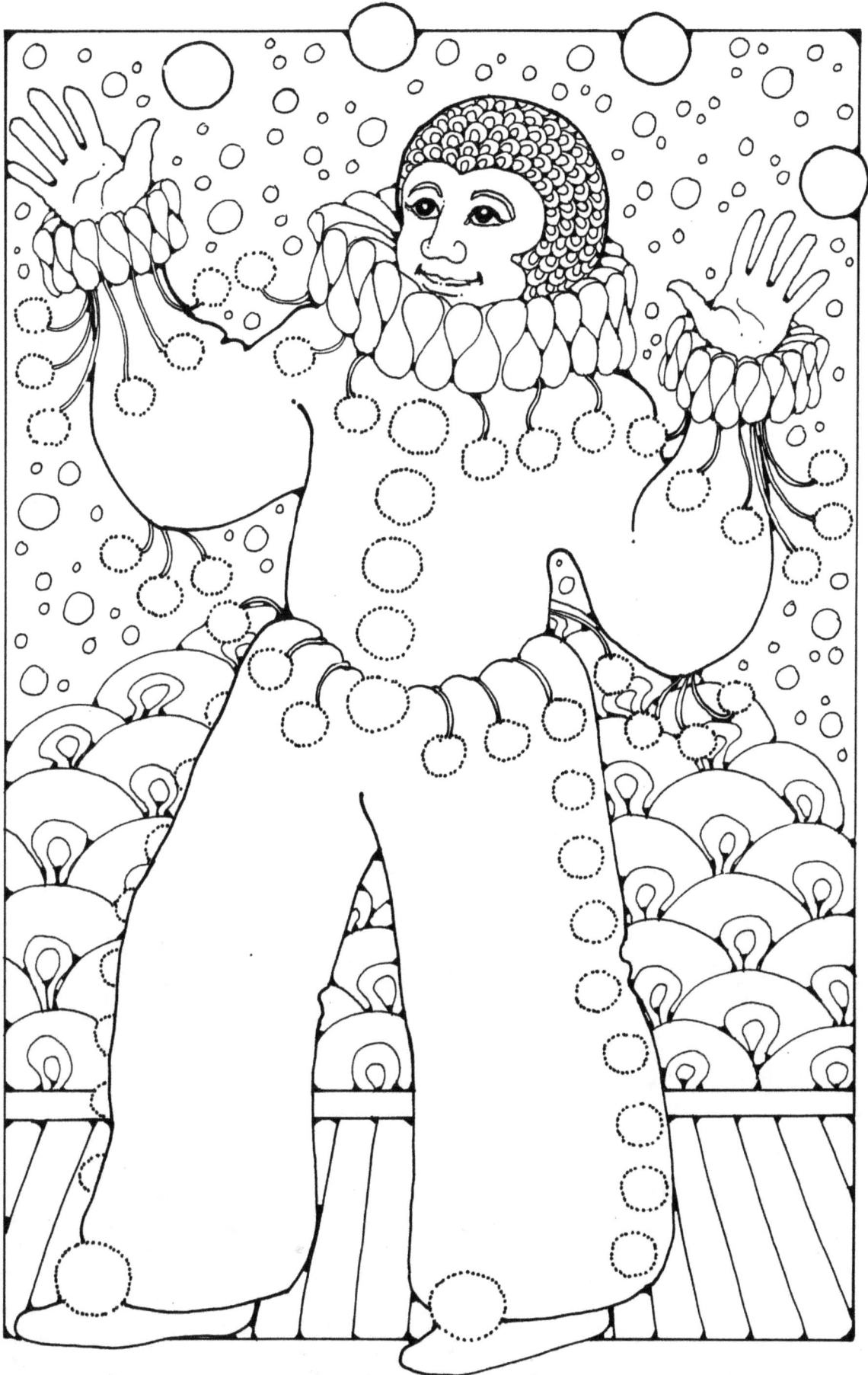

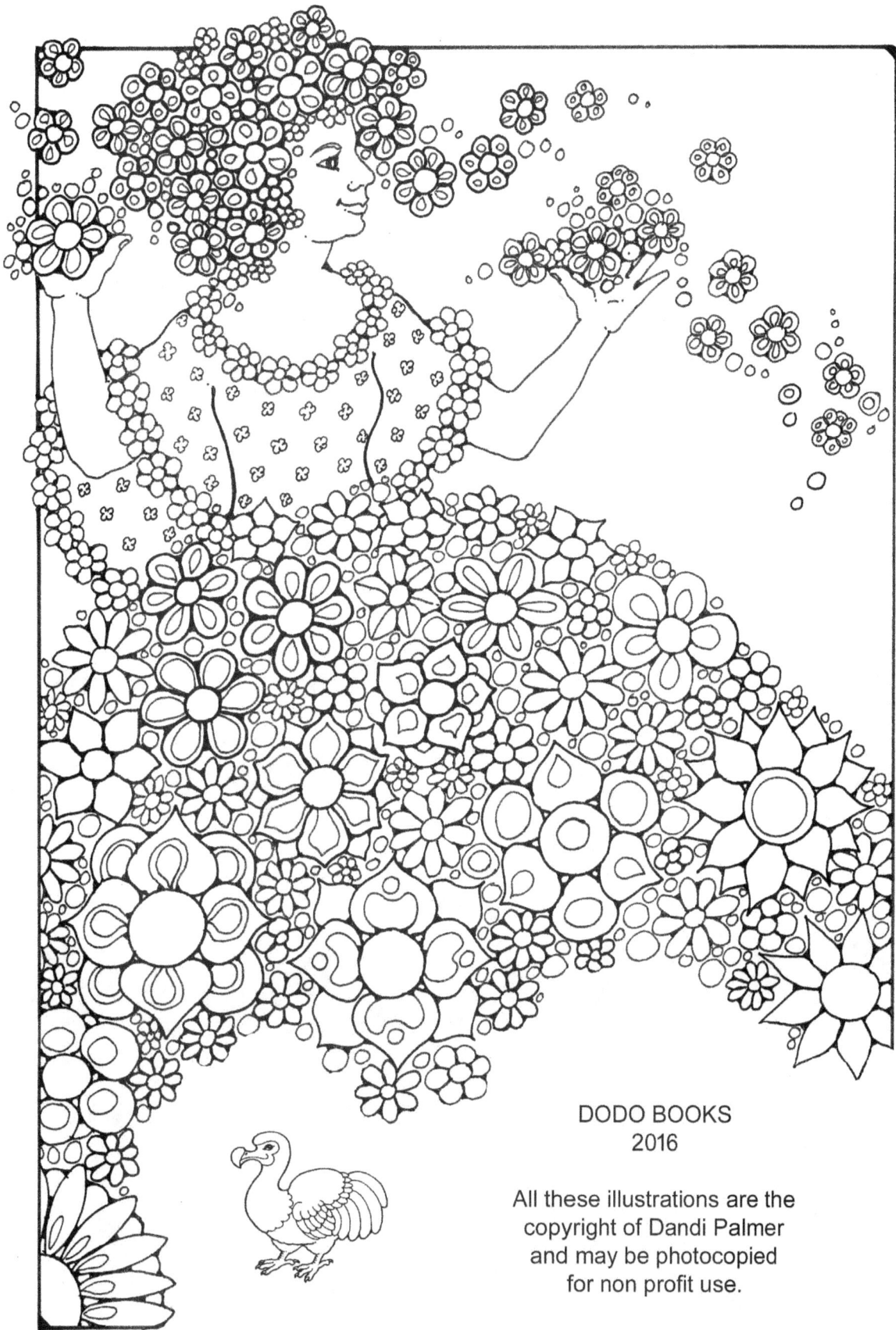

DODO BOOKS
2016

All these illustrations are the
copyright of Dandi Palmer
and may be photocopied
for non profit use.

www.ingramcontent.com/pod-product-compliance
Lightning Source LLC
Chambersburg PA
CBHW080216040426
42331CB00035B/3019